FIND
THAT
BIRD

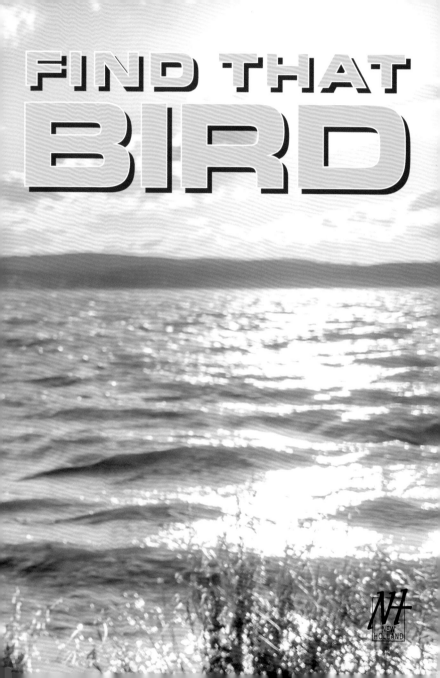

Contents

How To Find Birds

This handy introduction to Australian birds will help you to find and identify the different species you see, and enable you to tick them off as you go and keep a list.

Some species are hard to miss if you live in a town or city – for example Australian Magpies and Crested Pigeons are common in many parks and backyards all across the country, while Pacific Black Ducks and White-faced Herons are widespread on ponds, lakes and streams.

Other birds are specialists which are linked closely to particular habitats. You will very possibly find an oystercatcher on a rocky shoreline or a riflebird in a rainforest, but not vice versa. So visits to different habitats – forest, heath, woodland, lake, swamp, desert and coast – will produce new species.

Pay careful attention to the size of the bird, its shape and plumage, and where in the country it was seen. The birds in this book are widespread across Australia unless otherwise stated. For example, the Satin Bowerbird has a range encompassing 'E Australia' and therefore will not be seen near Darwin, Alice Springs or Perth.

If you get bitten by the birding bug it is well worth getting a comprehensive field guide such as the *Slater Field Guide to Australian Birds*, which will help you to recognise every species you see in any plumage. Using binoculars will enable you to watch birds more easily without disturbing them and therefore see more new species and get better views. And a digital camera with a good zoom can help with identification later on.

EMU

○ **Emu**
Huge and flightless.
Usually found away
from towns and cities,
often on plains or
in open woodland.
Stands 170cm tall.

WILDFOWL

○ **Magpie Goose**
Favours swamps and shallow lakes.
Forms big flocks. Can perch in trees.
N and E Australia. 80cm.

Black Swan

Distinctive large long-necked black waterbird with red bill. White wings obvious in flight. 125cm.

Plumed Whistling-Duck

Loud whistling calls and noisy wing-beats. Note long plumes on sides. Lakes in N and E Australia. 50cm.

Australian Wood Duck

Finely barred grey body and brown head. Lakes and swamps. Often grazes on short grass. Also called Maned Goose. 48cm.

Pacific Black Duck

Large brown duck with striped face. Common in all sorts of wetlands. Call a familiar *quack*. 54cm

Grey Teal

Small dabbling duck, common on all kinds of wetlands. Calls include *pip* and *quack*. 42cm.

Chestnut Teal

Male has distinctive red body and green head, female like Grey Teal but with darker head and throat. Wetlands in SW and SE Australia. 43cm.

Pink-eared Duck

Distinctive zebra-striped plumage and long bill. Has *chirrup* call. Found in all sorts of wetlands. 40cm.

Hardhead

Dives under water when feeding. Pale band at end of bill and white patch under tail. Male has white eye. Lakes. 47cm.

GREBES

● Australasian Grebe

Small waterbird that frequently dives to catch fish in lakes and ponds. Neck pale brown outside breeding season. Loud trilling call. 25cm.

● Great Crested Grebe

Elegant and long necked. Face and neck white outside breeding season. Ponds and lakes. 50cm.

BRUSH-TURKEY

● Australian Brush-turkey

Bare skin on head and neck. Builds huge
nest mounds where rotting vegetation
incubates eggs. Woodland in E Australia.
70cm.

DOVES AND PIGEONS

● Spotted Dove

Spotted necklace. Introduced
from Asia. Common in
towns and cities in E, SE
and SW Australia.
Song *coo-cook*.
27cm.

● **Brown Cuckoo-Dove**

Rusty-brown with long tail. Often quite tame. Forests in E Australia. 41cm.

● **Wonga Pigeon**

Blue-grey above with bold spots on white belly. Song *woo woo woo*. Forest and scrub in E Australia. 37cm.

Common Bronzewing

Iridescent bronze and green spots on wing. No crest. Common in forests and woodlands. 35cm.

Crested Pigeon

Tall spiky crest. Green and purplish spots on wings. Wings whistle in flight. Often in parks and gardens, also woodlands and forests. 33cm.

CUCKOOS

● Pheasant Coucal

Large clumsy cuckoo found
in grasslands with scrub.
Non-breeding plumage
streaked and mottled
brown all over. N and
E Australia. 62cm.

● Eastern Koel

Loud and persistent *coop-
coop-coop* call. Male plain
black, female spotted and
barred with white. Red eye.
Forests and gardens in N and
E Australia. 43cm.

Channel-billed Cuckoo

Large grey cuckoo with huge bill, long tail and loud squawking call. Feeds on figs. Forest and woodland in N and E Australia. 64cm.

Fan-tailed Cuckoo

Medium-sized cuckoo with chestnut breast. Lays eggs in nests of birds such as scrubwrens. Woodlands in S and E Australia. 26cm.

Shining Bronze-Cuckoo

Iridescent green and bronze above, barred below. Nest parasite of fantails and other small birds. Forest and woodland in S and E Australia. 18cm.

RAILS

Buff-banded Rail

Finely barred with brown stripes on head, rufous patch on breast and long pink bill. Swamps and wetlands. 31cm.

● Eurasian Coot

Plain grey-black with red eye, white bill and shield and lobed grey feet. Dives in lakes and wetlands to drag up pond weed. 37cm.

● Dusky Moorhen

Blackish with white undertail and red bill with yellow tip. Wetlands in E and SW Australia. 38cm.

Australasian Swamphen

Iridescent purple with white undertail, long pink legs and red bill and shield. Lakes and other wetlands. 48cm.

SHOREBIRDS

Masked Lapwing

Loud and conspicuous. Prominent yellow face wattle. Often seen in parks and on sports fields. 37cm.

○ **Black-fronted Dotterel**

Black-tipped red bill. Black stripe through eye and across breast. Common in wetlands across Australia. 17cm.

○ **Red-kneed Dotterel**

Black-tipped red bill. Black head and breast with extensive white throat. Lake edges and swamps. 18cm.

● Red-capped Plover

Pale brown above, plain white below. Male has rufous crown and neck-sides. Coasts and brackish water across Australia. 15cm.

● Red-necked Avocet

Fine upcurved bill and reddish head and neck. Black-and-white body. Nomadic visitor to shallow wetlands. 43cm.

● Pied Stilt

Outrageously long pink legs and narrow black bill. Very noisy *kip* calls. Shallow wetlands. 36cm.

● Pied Oystercatcher

Stout orange bill and stout pink legs. Loud piping calls often draw attention. Mainly coastal. 50cm.

● Eastern Curlew

Huge downcurved bill and streaked brown plumage. Coastal mudflats and estuaries. Call *cur-lee*. 57cm.

● Bar-tailed Godwit

Pale streaky brown plumage, turns reddish in breeding plumage. Long-distance migrant, breeds in Arctic. Mainly coastal. 42cm.

● Great Knot

Large pale grey sandpiper with a stout bill. Found around coasts on mudflats and beaches. 29cm.

● Sharp-tailed Sandpiper

Streaked shorebird with a reddish crown. Breeds in Siberia. Found in wetlands on coast and inland. 21cm.

● Red-necked Stint

Sparrow-sized. Pale grey and white with red neck in breeding plumage. Mainly coastal but often seen on inland wetlands. 15cm.

● Latham's Snipe

Cryptic plumage offers camouflage in well-vegetated swamps and wetlands. Breeds Japan. Migrant to E Australia. 25cm.

GULLS AND TERNS

● Silver Gull

Familiar coastal bird. Also occurs on inland wetlands and rubbish dumps. Bright red bill and legs. 40cm.

● Gull-billed Tern

Black bill. Black crown when breeding, black mask otherwise. Hunts over coastal and inland wetlands for fish and other prey. 39cm.

○ Caspian Tern

Huge tern with bright red 'carrot' bill. Seen along coasts and around inland wetlands. 56cm.

○ Crested Tern

Shaggy crest and narrow yellow-orange bill. Dives to catch fish in coastal waters around Australia. 46cm.

PENGUINS, TUBENOSES AND GANNETS

● Little Penguin

Bluish above, white
below. Oceanic waters
around southern coasts.
Comes ashore to breed
in burrows. 35cm.

● Wedge-tailed Shearwater

Stiff-winged gliding flight. Plain dark brown with diamond-
shaped tail. Seas around E and W Australia. 43cm.

Black-browed Albatross

Wingspan 220cm. Bill yellow in adult, blackish in immature.
Oceanic waters around southern half of Australia. 85cm.

Australasian Gannet

Adult white with yellow head and black tail and flight-
feathers. Dives spectacularly for fish in southern seas. 90cm.

DARTER AND CORMORANTS

● Pied Cormorant

Long grey bill and yellow skin around face. Dives to catch fish in lakes and sea. 73cm.

● Australian Darter

Known as 'snake bird' due to long sinuous neck. Bill dagger-like. Wetlands and coasts. 90cm.

Little Pied Cormorant

Short yellowish bill and lacks yellow skin above eye. Freshwater wetlands and coasts. 53cm.

Little Black Cormorant

Plain black with fine white plumes in breeding plumage. Staring green eye. Lakes, ponds and sheltered coastal waters. 63cm.

PELICAN AND HERONS

● Australian Pelican

Huge familiar black-and-white waterbird. Long bill with pouch for catching fish. Inland wetlands and coasts. 165cm.

● Great Egret

Plain white. Long bill and legs. Bill dark when breeding, yellow otherwise. Found in any wetland habitats. 84cm.

Cattle Egret

Plain white with short yellow bill. When breeding bill is reddish and plumage tinged buff. Wetlands and grasslands, especially with livestock. 50cm.

Striated Heron

Small greyish heron with yellow legs and dark crown. Juvenile heavily spotted. Coasts. 47cm.

● Nankeen Night Heron

Adult rufous with black crown. Juvenile brown, heavily spotted white. Nocturnal and crepuscular. Wetlands. 60cm.

● White-necked Heron

White head and neck, black body and bill. Found in wetlands throughout Australia. 88cm.

White-faced Heron

Medium-sized plain grey heron with yellow legs and white face. Common in all kinds of wetlands. 68cm.

CRANES

Brolga

Loud bugling call and spectacular dancing display. Long-legged. Grey with red band around neck. Marshes and grasslands in N and E Australia. 115cm.

IBISES AND SPOONBILLS

Australian Ibis

Ubiquitous in wetlands, grasslands and even city centres. Large downcurved bill. Mostly white with black head. 72cm.

Straw-necked Ibis

Similar to Australian Ibis but with glossy blackish wings and back. Shaggy white plumes on neck. Wetlands and grasslands. 68cm.

● Royal Spoonbill

White with black legs, face and spatulate bill. Can occur in all kinds of wetlands. 78cm.

● Yellow-billed Spoonbill

White with yellow legs and spoon-shaped bill, which is used to sift through shallow water for fish and invertebrate prey. 83cm.

BIRDS OF PREY

● Black-shouldered Kite

Often hovers while hunting. Small and whitish with black patches on wings. Open areas such as grasslands. 36cm.

● Whistling Kite

Pale brown. Soars often, when dark wing-tips are prominent. Found in open country. 53cm.

Black Kite

Distinctive V-shaped tail-fork visible in flight. Dark brown plumage. Can form large flocks. Open habitats. 52cm.

Collared Sparrowhawk

Dashing hunter of small birds. Adult has barred rufous underparts, juvenile streaked brown. Woodland. 35cm.

Wedge-tailed Eagle

Huge eagle with long diamond-shaped tail. Dark brown. Widespread in a variety of habitats. 95cm.

White-bellied Sea-Eagle

Broad winged and short tailed. Adult pale grey with black flight feathers. Juvenile mottled brown. Coasts and wetlands. 80cm.

● Nankeen Kestrel

Often hovers when hunting. Red-brown upperparts. Male has grey head and tail. Open woodland, plains. 33cm.

● Australian Hobby

Agile hunter of insects on the wing. Blue-grey above and buff below with black hood. Woodlands and plains. 32cm.

OWLS

● Barn Owl

Ghostly nocturnal hunter of
rodents. White facial disk with
black eyes. Loud hissing call.
Woodlands and plains. 33cm.

● Powerful Owl

Largest Australian owl. Often
feeds on possums. Barred dark
brown and white. Forests in E
and SE Australia. 62cm.

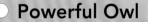

● Barking Owl

Call sounds like a barking dog. Dark brown spotted white above. Streaked breast. Open woodlands and forests. 40cm

● Southern Boobook

Small brown owl with onomatopoeic *book book* call. Woodlands, forests and sometimes parks and gardens. 32cm.

FROGMOUTHS, ROLLERS, BEE-EATERS AND KINGFISHERS

● **Tawny Frogmouth**

Cryptic plumage conceals this bird by day. At night actively hunts insects. Loud *oop oop* call. 40cm.

● **Dollarbird**

Often perches on dead tree or wire. Bluish with red bill and feet. Pale spot in each wing visible in flight. Forests in N and E Australia. 29cm.

Rainbow Bee-eater

Mainly green with black mask
and long central tail-streamers.
Orange wings obvious in flight.
Woodlands and plains. 23cm.

Azure Kingfisher

Dark blue above, orange
below. Hunts fish along
vegetated streams in
N and E Australia.
18cm.

Sacred Kingfisher

Blue-green above, cream below. Hunts insects and lizards in open wooded habitats. 21cm.

Red-backed Kingfisher

Similar to Sacred Kingfisher but whiter below and has streaked crown and red rump. Open woodland. 22cm.

● Laughing Kookaburra

Iconic large kingfisher known for its distinctive loud call. Found in open forest, parks and gardens in E and SW Australia. 46cm.

● Blue-winged Kookaburra

Close relative of Laughing Kookaburra, distinguished by plain greyish head and large blue patch on wing. Woodlands in N Australia. 43cm.

PARROTS

● Red-tailed Black Cockatoo

Large black cockatoo with red sides to tail. Patchy distribution in woodlands in N, E, W and central Australia. 56cm.

● Yellow-tailed Black Cockatoo

Large black cockatoo with yellow sides to tail and yellow patch on head. Woodlands and forests in E and SE Australia. 65cm.

Sulphur-crested Cockatoo

Familiar in parks and gardens as well as woodlands. White with long yellow crest. Loud screeching calls. N, E and SW Australia. 49cm.

Little Corella

Plain white with short crest and blue patch around eye. Woodland and parks. Often forms large flocks. 38cm.

● Galah

Bright pink with grey wings and tail. Forms noisy screeching flocks in woodlands and grasslands. 36cm.

● Cockatiel

Grey with long tail, white wing-patch and yellow-orange head with crest. Woodlands of Australian interior. 32cm.

Australian King-Parrot

Green above with orange-red belly.
Male has red head. Forests and
parks in E Australia. 43cm.

Crimson Rosella

Can become very tame in towns and parks. Bright red with
blue wings, tail and cheeks. Forests in E Australia. 34cm.

Rainbow Lorikeet

Familiar colourful garden bird
of E, SE and SW Australia.
Also in woodland and forest.
Often seen feeding on
blossom. 28cm.

Red-rumped Parrot

Small green parrot with blue
wings. Male brighter and has
red patch on rump. Woodland
in SE Australia. 27cm.

● Budgerigar

Popular pet. Wild birds are nomadic, forming large flocks in the Australian interior. Often seen near water. 18cm.

PITTAS

● Noisy Pitta

Shy ground-dwelling bird of forests in E Australia. Often detected by its call, which sounds like *walk to work*. 19cm.

BIRDS OF PARADISE, BOWERBIRDS, LYREBIRDS AND TREECREEPERS

● Paradise Riflebird

Blackish with patches of iridescent blue and green. Only in rainforests in SE Queensland and NE New South Wales. 29cm.

● Satin Bowerbird

Male glossy blue, female scalloped green, both have purple eye. Male decorates display 'bower' with blue objects. Forests in E Australia. 25cm.

● Superb Lyrebird

Amazing mimic of other birds' songs. Male fans remarkable tail during display. Often on woodland floor in SE Australia. 88cm.

● White-throated Treecreeper

Climbs up tree trunks. Grey-brown above with scaly belly. Woodlands and forests in E Australia. 14cm.

FAIRY-WRENS

● Red-backed Fairy-wren

Male black with red back, female plain pale brown. Woodlands in N and E Australia. 13cm.

● Variegated Fairy-wren

Male has bright blue head and tail, black breast and red patch on back. Female pale grey-brown with red around eye. Woodland. 15cm.

Superb Fairy-wren

Male black with electric blue patches on head and back, female plain brown with red around eye. Woodlands in E and SE Australia. 14cm.

Splendid Fairy-wren

Male bright blue with black lines. Female greyish with blue tail. Woodlands and scrub in W, S and central Australia. 14cm.

HONEYEATERS

● Eastern Spinebill

Grey and buff with a fine bill. Male with black band on breast. Woodlands and gardens in E and SE Australia. 15cm.

● Scarlet Honeyeater

Male bright red with black wings and tail. Female plain brown. Forests in E Australia. 11cm.

Lewin's Honeyeater

Distinctive 'machine gun' call. Plain greenish with yellow markings on head. Dense forest in E Australia. 20cm.

Singing Honeyeater

Black, yellow and white stripes on head. Yellow-green wings and tail. Woodlands and scrub. 20cm.

White-eared Honeyeater

Green with dark head and white patch behind eye. Forests and woodlands in S and E Australia. 20cm.

Yellow-faced Honeyeater

Greyish with yellow stripe on face bordered by black. Forest and woodland in E and SE Australia. 17cm.

White-plumed Honeyeater

Small with yellowish head, wings and tail. White tuft on side of head. Often seen along rivers. 17cm.

Blue-faced Honeyeater

Large with black head and white moustache. Blue skin on face, green in juvenile. Woodlands and forests in N and E Australia. 28cm.

White-throated Honeyeater

Small with white underparts and black head with white nape. Woodlands in N and E Australia. 14cm.

Brown-headed Honeyeater

Like a washed-out White-throated Honeyeater with a reddish eye-ring. Woodland in S Australia. 14cm.

● Bell Miner

Colonies obvious due to bell-like *tink* calls. Plain green with black face-markings. Forests and thickets in SE Australia. 19cm.

● Noisy Miner

Often in groups and aggressive to other birds. Familiar in many towns and cities. E and SE Australia. 27cm.

New Holland Honeyeater

White eye. Yellow patches on wings and tail. Heaths and woodlands in S Australia. 18cm.

White-cheeked Honeyeater

Like New Holland Honeyeater but white patch on cheek and dark eye. Heaths and woodlands in SW and E Australia. 18cm.

Tawny-crowned Honeyeater

Reddish crown and black stripe through eye extending down side. Heaths and woodlands in S Australia. 17cm.

Spiny-cheeked Honeyeater

Brown with pale buff throat and pink bill. Pale rump and white-tipped tail. Dry scrub. 25cm.

Red Wattlebird

Large and streaked with long tail, yellow belly and red wattle on cheek. Wooded areas, including in cities, in S Australia. 35cm.

Little Friarbird

Plain greyish with blue around eye. Woodland in N and E Australia. 27cm.

● Noisy Friarbird

Grey with bare black head
and white tail-tip. Loud
calls include *four o'clock*.
Forests and woodlands in
E Australia. 27cm.

BABBLERS

● White-browed Babbler

Usually in noisy flocks. Blackish
with white brow, throat and tail-tip.
Dry scrub in S Australia. 20cm.

PARDALOTES, SCRUBWRENS AND GERYGONES

● **Spotted Pardalote**

Tiny bird with delicately spotted plumage. Often high in trees. Wooded habitats in E and SW Australia. 9cm.

● **Striated Pardalote**

Tiny with yellowish brow, striped wings and yellow underparts and rump. Forests and woodlands. 10cm.

White-browed Scrubwren

Unobtrusive in dense undergrowth. White throat and brow and yellow eye. E, S and SW Australia. 12cm.

Brown Gerygone

Plain brown with grey breast and face and red eye. Damp forests and mangroves in E Australia. 10cm.

THORNBILLS, SILVEREYE AND SITELLA

● Brown Thornbill

Rufous crown and rump, streaked breast and red eye. Woodland and forest. 10cm.

● Striated Thornbill

Greenish. Head and breast finely streaked white. Woodland and scrub in E and SE Australia. 10cm.

● Silvereye

Bold white eye-eing. Conspicuous in wooded habitats including parks and gardens in E and SW Australia. 12cm.

● Varied Sitella

Seen in flocks. Hops along branches. Plumage variable according to sex and subspecies. Head can be black or white. Forests. 11cm.

CUCKOOSHRIKES, TRILLERS AND MONARCH FLYCATCHERS

Black-faced Cuckooshrike

Plain blue-grey with black face and long tail. Found in any habitat with trees. 33cm.

White-winged Triller

Plainish pale brown apart from breeding male which is black and white. Trilling song. Open woodland. 18cm.

Black-faced Monarch

Grey with black face and rufous belly. Damp forest in E Australia. 18cm.

Restless Flycatcher

Glossy black above with white throat, breast and belly. Often near water in woodlands. E and SW Australia. 20cm.

WHIPBIRDS, SHRIKE-TITS AND WHISTLERS

● Eastern Whipbird

Shy and skulking in dense damp forest in E Australia. Often best located by its loud 'whip-crack' song. 28cm.

● Crested Shrike-tit

Distinctive large black-and-white striped head. Isolated populations in E, SW and N Australia may represent different species. 18cm.

Golden Whistler

Male has black head and golden belly and collar. Female plain brownish. Whistling song. Forests in S and E Australia. 17cm.

Rufous Whistler

Grey with rufous belly. Male with black mask and breast-band. Loud song. Open forests. 17cm.

SHRIKE-THRUSHES, BELLBIRDS AND ORIOLES

● Grey Shrike-thrush

Plain greyish with brown back and white face. Common in forests and woodlands. 23cm.

● Crested Bellbird

Male has white face bordered black. Female plain greyish. Walks on ground in dry woodland. 22cm.

⬤ Olive-backed Oriole

Streaked grey and green with pink bill. Call *ori-ooo*.
Forest and woodland in N and E Australia. 27cm.

⬤ Figbird

Greenish. Male
with black
head and red
mask, female
with streaked
underparts. Fruit
trees in N and E
Australia. 28cm.

WOODSWALLOWS

● Dusky Woodswallow

Often in groups flying swallow-
like. Dark brown with pale
bill and white tail-
corners. Open
woodland. S and
E Australia.
18cm.

● Black-faced Woodswallow

Pale greyish with black
between bill and eye and
black tail. Chattering call.
Woodlands with grassy
understorey. 18cm.

● White-browed Woodswallow

Dark grey with white brow and rufous belly. Nomadic in dry open areas. 19cm.

● Masked Woodswallow

Grey with extensive mask – black in male, dark grey in female. Dry open woodlands. 19cm.

BUTCHERBIRDS, CURRAWONGS AND MAGPIE

- ## Australian Magpie

Large familiar bird. Famously will defend nest by dive-bombing. Beautiful fluty song. Woodlands and parks. 39cm.

- ## Pied Butcherbird

Like a small magpie with a white belly. So named because prey is impaled on branches. Open habitat with trees. 33cm.

Grey Butcherbird

Common in gardens and open woodlands. White underparts with black head and grey back. 30cm.

Pied Currawong

Black with long bill and white patches on wings, tail and undertail. Forms large flocks in winter. Wooded places in E Australia. 46cm.

FANTAILS AND MISTLETOEBIRD

Willie Wagtail

Characterful and confiding. Will fearlessly defend nest against much larger predators. Many habitats, including cities. 20cm.

Grey Fantail

Conspicuous and restless, often fanning long tail. Any habitat with trees, including parks and gardens. 16cm.

Rufous Fantail

Long tail frequently fanned. Bright reddish brow and rump. Damp forest in E Australia. 16cm.

Mistletoebird

Tiny with short bill. Male black with red throat and undertail. Female greyish. Found anywhere with mistletoe plants. 10cm.

MAGPIE-LARK, CHOUGH, RAVENS AND FLYCATCHERS

● Magpie-lark

Confiding. Often walks on ground. Builds mud nest. Call *pee-o-wit*. Open habitats, including parks and gardens. 27cm.

● White-winged Chough

Often walks in groups on ground in open forest. Red eye and downcurved bill. White wing-patches visible in flight. E Australia. 45cm.

Australian Raven

Large and glossy black with white eye and loud wailing call. Varied habitats, including cities, in E and SW Australia. 52cm.

Jacky Winter

Makes sallying flights to catch insects. Plain greyish with white outer tail-feathers. Open woodland. 13cm.

ROBINS

Scarlet Robin

Male pied with bright red breast and white forehead. Female similar but paler. Open woodland in SW and SE Australia. 13cm.

Red-capped Robin

Similar to Scarlet Robin but male has red forehead. Female paler brownish. Dry woodlands. 12cm.

● Eastern Yellow Robin

Often very confiding in woodlands and forests in E Australia. Grey with yellow underparts and rump. 15cm.

● Hooded Robin

Black and white wings and tail. Male with black head, female grey. Dry woodland. 16cm.

REED WARBLERS, SWALLOWS, MARTINS AND SWIFTS

● Australian Reed Warbler

Inhabits reedbeds. Plain pale brown with loud song of repeated phrases. 17cm.

● Welcome Swallow

Glossy blue above with red face. Forked tail with long streamers. Twittering song. Often nests under eaves or bridges. 15cm.

● Fairy Martin

Like a short-tailed swallow with
a white rump and throat and
reddish crown. Open woodland.
12cm.

● White-throated Needletail

Strong flight on scythe-shaped wings.
Does not perch. White on throat, undertail
and back. E Australia. 20cm.

PIPITS, THRUSHES AND STARLINGS

Australasian Pipit

Upright slender streaky brown bird of open grasslands and dunes. Runs on ground rather than hopping. 16cm.

Bassian Thrush

Shy inhabitant of damp forests in E Australia. Heavily barred plumage and warbling song. 27cm.

● Common Starling

Introduced from Europe. Now common in E Australia.
Glossy blackish with white spots. Often in flocks. 21cm.

● Common Myna

Introduced from Asia,
now common in cities and
hinterlands in E Australia.
Note yellow face and bill and
white wing-patches. 24cm.

FINCHES

● Chestnut-breasted Mannikin

In flocks in grassland in N and E Australia. Black face and chestnut breast and tail. 10cm.

● Zebra Finch

Reddish bill and cheek and 'zebra stripes' on breast and tail. Dry grassland and woodland. 10cm.

◯ Double-barred Finch

White breast with two black bands. Spotted wings. Open woodland in N and E Australia. 11cm

◯ Red-browed Finch

Grey with green wings and red bill, brow and rump. Forms flocks in woodlands and mangroves in E Australia. 12cm.

Other bird species seen...

○ _____   ○ _____

○ _____   ○ _____

○ _____   ○ _____

○ _____   ○ _____

○ _____   ○ _____

○ _____   ○ _____

○ _____   ○ _____

○ _____   ○ _____

○ _____   ○ _____

○ _____   ○ _____

○ _____   ○ _____

○ _____   ○ _____

○ _____   ○ _____

○ _____   ○ _____

○ _____   ○ _____

Image Credits

All photos from Shutterstock.com – individual photographer names as follows
(a = above, b = below, l = left, r = right):

Abhi Photo Village, page 15b; Agami Photo Agency, pages 10b, 19a, 21a, 24a, 24b, 25ar, 28b; Alec Trusler2015, page 48b; Alexandr Junek Imaging, page 50b; Alybaba, page 85a; Anne Powell, pages 60b, 80b; Ashley Whitworth, page 65b; Banonili, page 12b; Barnaby Chambers, page 13a; Belle Ciezak, page 56b; Bird Dude, page 90a; Birdiegal, pages 23a, 37a; Braden Mitchell, page 33b; Bryan Pollard, page 91a; Cezary Wojtkowski, page 35b; Chris Ison, pages 36b, 58a, 66b, 68b, 72br; Chris Morecroft, pages 72bl, 74b; Christopher Robin Smith Photography, page 47a; Chris Watson, pages 14a, 57b; Cola Cat, page 6a; Colorfeel, page 72a; Cristian Gusa, page 7a; Daniel Pertovt, page 34b; David Roy Carson, page 73b; David Steele, pages 11b, 26a, 32b, 34a, 37b, 44a, 59b; Dennis Jacobsen, page 52a; Devin Hunt, pages 45a, 73a; Diverse, page 49a; Dr Ajay Kumar Singh, page 26b; Ecopix, page 83a; Elizabeth Caron, page 38a; Eugene Drobitko, page 30 br; Feathercollector, pages 15a, 25b, 53b, 84b; Frank McClintock, pages 65a, 88a; G-Hep, page 61b; Gary Thomas Photography, page 16b; Gregory J Smith, page 90b; Greg Wyncoll, page 68a; Harold Stiver, page 8a; Hayley Alexander, page 57a; Ian Peter Morton, page 53a; Imagevixen, page 49b; Imogen Warren, pages 9a, 10a, 11a, 18b, 20a, 23b, 27b, 33al, 54a, 55b, 59a, 62a, 63a, 66a, 69a, 69b, 70a, 70b, 77a, 78a, 79a; Jan Danek, page 18a; Janelle Lugge, page 39a; Jason Benz Bennee, pages 58b, 71a, 84a; Jocelyn Watts, page 22b; John Carnemolla, page 50a; Jonathan Steinbeck, pages 36a, 44b; Jonathan Tickner, page 64a; Jukka Jantunen, pages 14b, 20b, 83b; Juliasimages, page 19b; Katarina Christenson, pages 75a, 86a; Katyne Wee, page 46a; Ken Griffiths, pages 9b, 16a, 30bl, 33ar, 41a, 54br, 55a, 64b, 80a, 81b, 82b; Lameh, page 48a; Lena Viridis, pages 2-3; Luke Shelley, pages 21b, 40a, 52b, 74a; Man Down Media, page 93b; Mandy Creighton, page 31a; Mari May, page 54bl; Mark Higgins, page 30a; Martin Mecnarowski, page 47b; Martin Pelanek, page 82a; Martin Prochazkacz, page 22a; Massimiliano Paolino, page 42a; Maurizio de Mattei, page 61a; Merrillie Redden, page 88b; Michal Pesata, page 43b; Michal Sloviak, page 13b; Mxk Russ, page 77b; Natalia van D, pages 1, 92a; Nicolette Coombs, page 45b; Nik Mark Mulconray, page 76b; Pete Evans, pages 17a, 56a, 92a, 93a; Peter 6172, page 46b; Phillip Allaway, page 51a; Rajh Photography, page 43a; Raymond Chung Photography, page 87b; Robert J Richter, page 27a; Rock Ptarmigan, page 25al; Russ Jenkins, pages 12a, 85b; Sahara Prince, page 35a; Scott Mirror, page 89b; Sirtravelalot, page 32a; SJ Duran, pages 8b, 63b; Sompreaw, page 87a; Stubblefield Photography, page 91b; Sunreal, page 29b; Susan Flashman, pages 6b, 75b; Timothy Christianto, page 89a; Trevor Scouten, page 42b; Uwe Bergwitz, page 51b; Victor Baril, page 28a; Vladimir Strnad, page 29a; Wang LiQuiang, page 17b; Wayne Butterworth, page 31b; Whitejellybeans, page 67a; Wright Out There, pages 7b, 38b, 39b, 41b, 60a, 62b, 67b, 71b, 76a, 78b, 79b, 81a, 86b; YapAhock, page 40b.

First published in 2022 by Reed New Holland Publishers
Sydney

Level 1, 178 Fox Valley Road, Wahroonga, NSW 2076, Australia

newhollandpublishers.com

A record of this book is held at the National Library of Australia.

ISBN 978 1 92158 052 9

Managing Director: Fiona Schultz
Publisher and Project Editor: Simon Papps
Designer: Andrew Davies
Production Director: Arlene Gippert

Printed in China

10 9 8 7 6 5 4 3 2 1

Also available from Reed New Holland:

Find That Bug ISBN 978 1 92158 053 6

Chris Humfrey's Awesome Australian Animals ISBN 978 1 92554 670 5

Chris Humfrey's Coolest Creepy Crawlies ISBN 978 1 76079 445 3

For details of hundreds of other Natural History titles see
newhollandpublishers.com

Keep up with New Holland Publishers and ReedNewHolland:
 NewHollandPublishers
 @newhollandpublishers